MW00466124

You Wouldn't Want an
OSTRICH
for Your
MAMA!

Concepts in Disciple-making

CARLTON L. COON, SR.

You Wouldn't Want an Ostrich for Your Mama!
Concepts in Disciple-making

By Carlton L. Coon, Sr.

© 2011 United Pentecostal Church International

All rights reserved. Duplication of material in this book is not permitted without prior permission of the author.

All Scriptures are from the King James Version unless otherwise noted.

Printed in the United States of America

CONTENTS

Chapter 1:
The Bottom Line: Make Disciples!

Disciple-making is not an option—it is the end product of the church. New birth and church attendance are essential processes in the creation of the end product; however, a church can have large Sunday attendance, have many converts, and not be developing disciples for Jesus Christ. Some observations run contrary to preferred experience. Will you trust me enough to hear my experience?

Some years ago, my life changed from being a pastor to serving as General Director of the Home Missions Division of the United Pentecostal Church International. My first meeting with the Home Missions Administrative Committee included me sharing a bit of history. History is important because it is the shaping influence of the present. In 1992, our family moved to Springfield, Missouri, to assume a pastorate. The church's average attendance for the prior Sundays had been eighty-five. Morale was low. Faithful people were weary, disenfranchised, and somewhat frustrated.

The church's growth was interesting. We didn't break any records. For years, nobody paid much attention. Our early years' focus was to heal and resurrect hope. Hopeless saints cannot effectively minister to the community around them.

My first numerical goal: let's baptize an average of one per month. Not much faith there you say, but... well, it sort of depends on where you are coming from. About the second year into our being on-site, we accomplished that particular goal.

Immediately, there was a new target, "We've come this little distance; could we baptize an average of one per week?" It happened! Not suddenly, for several years we kept inching toward the goal. Finally we made it. Again, the target changed, "Suppose we could baptize an average of two per week?" It happened the same year we laid out the challenge—that very year 105 were baptized in Jesus' name.

It makes a good testimony. Now, you need to hear how it happened. In the process of growth, the church never had a "100-soul revival." The most we ever baptized in one night was eight. You may say, "That sure doesn't measure up to some of the things I hear about." No argument here. We accomplished far too little. Others had much more notable happenings—events to be lauded and celebrated.

Now back to the discussion of disciple-making. During the same years, a friend's pastorate had over three hundred receive the Holy Ghost in one revival. Interesting—in the particular situation, a year later no more people were attending church or serving God than before the revival.

Making disciples or the lack thereof is personal. Evangelist Samuel Chadwick blamed himself for letting some new converts get into a church that was cold and apathetic about caring for them, Chadwick's self-indictment, "It was like putting a new baby in the arms of a corpse."

John Wesley stormed at his preachers in training, "How dare you lead people to Christ without providing opportunity for growth and nurture! Anything less than growth and nurture is simply begetting children for the murderer."

Some decades ago a church had a phenomenal ingathering. Nine hundred received the Holy Ghost. A year later the passionate pastor had those stand who had received the Holy Ghost in that series of meetings. One person stood... ONE! One! You read it right: ONE! With obvious dismay at the breakdown in accomplishing the commission of the Lord Jesus Christ, that pastor led his church to adjust its focus to put as much effort into the process of discipling converts as they had into birthing those converts.

News reports in October 2007 had pop star Britney Spears losing her parental rights. What behavior causes one to lose such rights? Might there be a spiritual analogy between Ms. Spears' parental care (or the lack thereof) and the church's care of a convert? Does God ever revoke a church's rights to be spiritual parents?

In Jack Cunningham's book *Planting Daughter Churches* he noted, "A great foreign missionary once told me that church growth is nothing more or less than retention! You can have many people come through the doors of the church, but if you are not learned in the art of disciple-making, you will lose as many out the back door as come through the front door."

Why Discipleship Fails

1. <u>We diminish the significance of the baby we have, in pursuit of the one yet to be born.</u> We see the opportunities of the many *en masse*, rather than to see the possibility that exists in a single life. Our thinking becomes, "If only God would send us a dozen or a hundred in a revival, we'd really do something to care for them." Question: What are you doing to take care of the one or two converts

God has already given you? The Lord Jesus Christ never provides salvation wholesale. It is always retail—the full price of redemption being paid and the necessary resources for an individual's development being provided. Those who make disciples understand what Sam Shoemaker was saying, "Men are not hewn out of the mediocre mass wholesale, but one by one." Just as parenting happens one child at a time, disciples are made one person at a time.

2. <u>The grand is more attractive than the consistent.</u> Our back yard had a wonderful pear tree. It is at its most beautiful when covered with blooms. Blooms don't sell—fruit does. At the end of the harvest, it's the mature fruit that counts. An abundant harvest not brought into the barn gives little satisfaction and no revenue. Is it possible to expend time, money, and energy on a grand thing that is of little lasting impact? Do some of our staged events attract church-men but do little to attract or connect with the unsaved? A year later, does any fruit remain?

3. <u>Disciple-making is hard work.</u> For most, it is much easier to preach a sermon, sing a solo, host a special meeting, build a new building, or plan and carry out a "Friend Day" than to plan, establish, and consistently do the behind the scenes work of disciple-making. Discipleship is roll-up-your-sleeves hard work.

Now a return to the brief history. If there was not an epoch-making event or series of events, how did we grow? God led us to focus on an intense effort to keep alive and growing those we saw born again. Our growth pattern was not the hullabaloo of an event, but the consistent hard work of effectively operating a spiritual nursery. The result was steady "disciple-able" growth. When consistently with each breath the church is exhaling disciples, it will also consistently inhale new converts. God has called us to help people get to heaven.

When we came to Springfield, God spoke, "If you want spiritual babies, build a spiritual nursery. I'm not going to send you babies till you do." From that word was birthed a philosophy—one I later discovered was inherent in the New Testament. Disciple-making is the bottom line of the work of a church. If you are going to invest in an event or into a process of making disciples, choose to invest in making disciples.

I remember sitting around a folding table with a little think tank. Some of those involved included Diane Rose, Bob and Jeri Burk, and Lee and Debbie Suttles. In our meeting we talked about what a new convert needs when they come to God. What are their challenges? What are their issues? What are the things they will struggle with?

That first brainstorming session only led to more questions...

- How do we respond to those challenges, issues, and struggles? To know an infant needs special care is not the same thing as responding to a baby's needs.

- What specific actions can we take to make sure spiritual babies are being taken care of to the best of our abilities?

- What processes do we need to establish to make sure this effort is not "hit and miss?"

- What difference will our specific actions make?

Let me stir you to thought. This is not a zero-sum matter; one does not have to choose one or the other. But which would you choose if you could have only one of the following two things happen:

Option #1
In the next twelve months your church could have a great harvest. Two hundred fifty people receive the Holy Ghost. It is heralded. Publications discuss the revival. Others come to observe. Awards are presented... One year later five of those people are attending church and growing in Christian maturity.

Option #2
In the coming year twenty-five receive the Holy Ghost. Nobody outside the local church pays much attention. What has happened does not remotely rival the Day of Pentecost. No articles are written... no awards presented. One year later seven of those people are attending church and continuing to grow in Christ.

Which of those two experiences is the nearest to Jesus' purpose of getting people to heaven? What is the real point? Disciple-making should happen whether many or few are receiving the Holy Ghost.

Faithful men and women can become disillusioned when their church's revival does not match someone else's. Is it possible we frustrate ourselves? In spite of the race not being to the swift, the accolades still go to the swift. Yet in reality, many disciple-making churches and pastors never get much applause or credit. God has called us to make disciples not converts. Conversion is the first wonderful step of development.

For Further Contemplation

Consider all of this a bit more...

- How many were born again in your church last year? Three years ago? Five years ago?

- How many of them are serving God today?

- Were those babies given the same care a baby in the natural received?

- There may be a nursery for the saint's kids; do you have a spiritual nursery outfitted for the born again?

- Is it possible for a baby to starve in the presence of good healthy food? Would you feed a two-week-old a steak? Would you feed a two-week-old spiritual baby a ninety-minute Bible study on the silver sockets in the tabernacle in the wilderness? Would they understand it and be built up? Did the newcomer get any more spiritual nutrition from last week's Bible study or sermon than the two-week-old would get from the steak?

What Now?

What can you do about what you just diagnosed? Think of three practical steps you could take to care and build up the newest members of your church. You may even want to speak with your pastor about specific roles needed in the church to best care for guests.

Are you willing to invest as much effort into discipleship as you have put into converting them? Hospitals are expensive and the pain of delivery intense, but the greater cost of time, money, and (in some instances) parental effort, comes after birth rather than before. This is the normal. Conversion is five percent; following up the decision to repent, be baptized, and receive the Holy Ghost is ninety-five percent.

And remember: whether you have a formal role on your church's staff or not, the task of making disciples is *everyone's* job and takes the entire church. The pastor is certainly in charge of the hospital, but it takes a full staff in the delivery room and a caring family at home to raise a child. Your pastor needs your help to make sure a new convert isn't stranded after a "delivery room" conversion experience.

Jack Cunningham's missionary friend had it right: "You can't grow His kingdom or the local church if you do not close the back door!"

Indeed!

Chapter 2:
The Problem with Ostriches

Turning converts into disciples closes the "back door" of the church. Listen to two voices:

Paul Graham pastors in Montreal, Canada. Some years ago he wrote, "In 1985, God dealt with me to start Discipleship classes. I did the classes until someone else was trained. Over the past twenty years those who go through Discipleship classes have about a 75% retention rate. Many become involved in some ministry. We retain less than 20% of those who don't take a Discipleship class. And of those who do stay, they do not grow spiritually—just become basic Sunday morning bench warmers. Over the years we have broken the barriers of 100, 200, 300, 400, and 500. We now occasionally bump over the 600 mark in Sunday attendance. Discipleship has been the key. We don't keep them all, but it is much better than before."

Retired Elder William Cass said, "In a revival we had 28 receive the Holy Ghost. A short time later only a few were still attending. I wondered why! What I missed and apparently many others miss was "discipling those converts." Since that time I have taught many New Convert Classes. A large percentage of those who attended are still living for the Lord. Fortunately, I woke up in time to save many a soul who probably would have fallen away for lack of discipleship."

Strange title: "You wouldn't want an ostrich for your mama!" Trust me—you really wouldn't! The Bible actually discusses it:

Gavest thou the goodly wings unto the peacocks? or wings and feathers unto the ostrich? Which leaveth her eggs in the earth, and warmeth them in dust, And forgetteth that the foot may crush them, or that the wild beast may break them. She is hardened against her young ones, as though they were not hers: her labour is in vain without fear; Because God hath deprived her of wisdom, neither hath he imparted to her understanding. What time she lifteth up herself on high, she scorneth the horse and his rider (Job 39:13-18).

An ostrich is impressive:

- A mature ostrich stands over six feet tall: "she lifteth herself up on high."

- An ostrich can outrun a horse for short distances: "she scorneth the horse."

Yes, an ostrich is impressive, but an ostrich isn't much of a mama. Her behavior toward her young denotes her lack of wisdom and understanding. An ostrich moves fast and stands tall—impressive things that catch the eye—but she is not a pattern for maturing spiritual babies.

A young ostrich's survival depends on chance. Maybe... perhaps... possibly... the chick will survive. There is no personal responsibility from a parent. The young ostrich's uncertain odds of survival are the result of poor mothering. Several qualities and habits impair an ostrich's parenting skills:

- An ostrich drops her eggs in the desert dust. No nest. Nothing—just another day in the life of a bad mama. No special preparations are made. The chicks are at risk; accident or intent may destroy them.

Well now... what does the "nest" for your church's spiritual babies look like? Is there a safe place for them to grow and be fed a diet they can digest? Where do they have a chance to ask questions—and not be treated as though their questions are foolish? How are they protected from accidental or intentional damage?

We hope for the best, but what *intentional* actions are we taking on behalf of spiritual babies? Spiritual babies don't want an ostrich for their mama.

- An ostrich leaves her young behind. The mother has something else to do. Perhaps there is a horse to race or someone to impress with how tall she stands. Some activity is more important than her young.

What is so important that a mother abandons her young? Shouldn't a good mother be constantly busy responding to the needs of her little one?

Where do you spend your time? How long since you personally spent time with a new-born Christian? What fulfills you? Are you okay with having babies and then wondering whether they lived or died?

- An ostrich is hardened against her young. It is as though they were not her own.

Interesting word: "hardened." A mother ostrich feels no emotional attachment. She feels no sense of loss if an animal eats her young. She can still run fast and stand tall. It is as though her chicks were strangers. Does she see her baby as competition for available food?

Do we care about spiritual babies with anything approaching the intensity we feel for our natural offspring? Does anyone feel a sense of responsibility for them and a passion to protect them?

- The labor she expends to lay the eggs is labor that is in vain.

Sound familiar? Great resources are expended on the egg being laid and a baby being born. There is celebration in the delivery room. Saints rejoice over the wonder of new birth. Is the baby then forgotten? Do we get so busy *conceiving* the next thing that we forgot to care for the last thing?

Now for some discomfort—how much does your involvement and mothering style in your local church resemble that of an ostrich? What are you going to do about it? An unscientific observation seems to indicate we have more "ostrich" churches in North America than we have "mothering" churches. Eternal destiny depends on more than having experienced a new birth; we need to remake the ostrich.

Remaking an Ostrich

What would change? Almost everything:

- Become extremely sensitive to the needs of spiritual babies. A mother is attuned to the slightest whimper of her offspring. She can hear distress that everyone else ignores.

- Accept responsibility! Paul told the saints at Thessalonica that he cared for them "like a mother caring for children." He understood the relationship. The maturing of people became personal to him.

- Create a safe place. You probably won't call your Discipleship efforts, "The Nest," but that is what Disciple-making should provide.

- If your survival rate is low, do something different. Be aggressive enough to learn from someone who is doing a better job with spiritual parenting.

- Invest as much energy into caring for and developing spiritual babies as you do getting them born-again.

The Bible has a number of other illustrations of the sad things that can happen to the young.

Lamed by a Caregiver

Remember Mephibosheth, who lived his life under the provision and protective care of King David. How did he end up a dependent?

> And Jonathan, Saul's son, had a son that was lame of his feet. He was five years old when the tidings came of Saul and Jonathan out of Jezreel, and his nurse took him up, and fled: and it came to pass, as she made haste to flee, that he fell, and became lame. And his name was Mephibosheth (2 Samuel 4:4).

Mephibosheth was lame because of his caregiver's hurry. Her hurry became his harm. No impairment came to her because of her haste. Mephibosheth survived but was forever handicapped by her hurry.

Making disciples cannot be rushed. There has to be a progressive revelation of God. Think of how little the average new convert actually knows about God and the Bible. Giving that new believer the knowledge base to become what they can become takes time.

With that limited knowledge clearly in mind, imagine a Harvard math professor leaving his position to go teach algebra to children in kindergarten. His progress and that of the children would be limited. The failure would not be because of his lack of knowledge, but the mind of a five-year-old is not prepared to deal with higher math. Math depends on a progressive education. Kids have to learn to add, subtract, multiply, and divide; then comes fractions and decimals. Finally they have the ability to deal with the science of figures. What would have been difficult becomes easy, but the math professor can't rush the process.

In a similar way we deal with the process of making disciples. If you hurry them, you will harm them. I'm not talking about ignoring their development... invest in the new baby at their level of understanding. Don't load them with the responsibilities of mature Christianity when they have not yet finished kindergarten. Discern, validate, and appreciate the significance of spiritual babies.

Can I just speak plainly: we tend to fear when there are babies under our care. These spiritual infants are not yet living up to certain lifestyle expectations. Does that sort of fear make as much sense as a couple with their newborn being afraid of being criticized if their newborn dirties a diaper? Don't harm a spiritual baby out of fear of what someone else might think of you—the caregiver. Spiritual babies should not be put in harm's way. Some have been permanently impaired because we hurried through what should have been a deliberate process.

<u>Direction for Spiritual Nurses</u>

- Don't fear outside pressure. New converts are not to be hurried to responsibilities they are not ready for.

- As a saint, encourage and equip new babies for an ongoing personal relationship with Jesus Christ. Show them by example basic, daily things of Christian life, personal quiet times, the disciplines of prayer and fasting, church attendance, and how to reach out to their friends.

- Take your time. Be deliberate. How long does it take to develop a disciple? My personal estimate: with a focused Discipleship effort, it takes anywhere from three to five years. Ostrich churches will keep a few of their newborn, but unfortunately they grow up to be just like the mama that birthed them.

- Be careful with spiritual babies not to get in a rush. Sometimes saints who have been in the church for fifteen years want to hold a new believer up to the same expectations they are now living. Such will hurt

19

these babies. Remember that they need your help and be reasonable in your expectations.

Threatened by Babies

People can tell if you want them around. It isn't verbiage; it's behavior. Pharaoh and Herod lived in different eras, but both were motivated by fear. Herod and Pharaoh became threatened by infants. Each newborn Hebrew was a threat. Pharaoh and Herod's remedy: if it is a threat, kill it.

An average church operates on a delicate balance. People sit on those same seats at the end of a pew (where a guest has to climb over them) every service. Social groups are clearly defined. New people threaten the delicate balance of the average church.

Now... I know your church is far more spiritual than what I'm describing. You are thinking, "Social groupings and positioning does not come into play in our church." Okay, as an experiment, what if your pastor announced that for the next three weeks, he had decided to have someone else do your job and lead the praise, teach Sunday school, pass out bulletins, or whatever it is you normally do each week? What if he even asked you to sit on a different pew than where you normally do? You may well discover how position comes into play.

Being threatened by new spiritual babies may not enter into a pastor's thinking, but it affects the behavior of saints. Churches—even young Home Missions congregations— become closed social sets. In an average church in North America, everybody knows everybody. New spiritual babies are fearful things. "Will they get more attention from the pastor? What if she is a better keyboardist? I hear he sings—does he sing better than me?" You know the things I'm talking about.

One can only break into a closed social set with much effort. I am talking about the "kicking and screaming" kind of exertion. Most new converts don't have it in them.

An elder tells of a new pastor who led his church to growth; soon there was some trouble. One of the "old" saints commented, "We had a good little church till all these new people started coming!"

In a research project, church dropouts were asked two questions:

1. Why did you drop out?

2. What would most influence your choice of a new church home?

The answer most commonly given to the first question was, "I did not feel part of the group." The response to the second question (almost 75 percent), was "the friendliness of the next church's people." How we respond in welcoming newcomers and making them feel a sense of "place" is important.

Remedy for Fearing the Baby

*   The pastor and church leaders have to be highly visible in spending time with new converts. Are you in a role of leadership at the church? Are you an active saint? Are you visible around the church? If so, you especially have the eyes on the new convert upon you. Have coffee with them. Invite them to your home. Demystify yourself to them. Be an example to others on the need to get to know the baby.

*   Establish an open door approach. One of the longest words Jesus ever used was "whosoever." The

word He seemed to like the best was "come." Jesus' idea: "whosoever will, let him come." He aggressively welcomed all sorts of people. Be open to people who are different from you; a different skin tone, different first language, different social background—work at it till it becomes natural.

- Learn to hug new people. Tell them, "I love you! I'm glad you are here. Thank you for being part of our church." Even before babies understand words, they recognize the meaning conveyed by the outstretched arms of a mother. What is being conveyed by your posture?

- Draw other people into the fellowship circle and slowly coach them that these spiritual babies are why the church exists.

- Don't turn the "closed social set" into a squabble. While others may resent new converts in words or attitudes, change it with your behavior and leadership as a member of the church family—a family that loves, welcomes, and cares for everyone.

Chapter 3:
Building a Hothouse

Did you know you can start tomato plants in the dead of winter—if you build a "hothouse." The hothouse is not the tomato plant's final destination, but it's the environment in which they start. Plants grown in a hothouse are eventually "hardened off," but they get their start in a controlled environment.

You don't have the option of sequestering a convert, but your church can provide a "hothouse" in which young Christians develop. Jesus understood how things grow and develop: "For the earth bringeth forth fruit of herself; first the blade, then the ear, after that the full corn in the ear" (Mark 4:28).

For there to be full corn in the ear, a plant has to survive being a "blade." New converts are "blades" to nurture. The farmer's goal is never the "blade"; it is always the "full corn in the ear," but it has to start somewhere.

A nurturing environment responds to the dangers of the current climate. Are you part of a "hothouse" designed to nurture the spiritually young.

Climate Condition #1 – Life Perspective

In North America *self* is enthroned. Entitlement and pleasure are attendants in the throne room. Those we are hoping to evangelize have more "stuff" than any generation but are unsatisfied. They seek the spiritual. Their search for the spiritual takes on several different levels of intensity.

Some want the spiritual as <u>an addendum</u> to an already over-stuffed life.

Others want to experience the spiritual as though it were a thrill-ride—a thing to experience and move on. They want an <u>encounter but not a life-change</u>. For such new converts, Christ's kingdom holds little lasting value.

Many are <u>sincere</u>... and so desperate for change that God, God's Word, and His church become a lifeline of hope. These you can develop.

We battle a mindset as we work to transition the spiritually newborn from being self-absorbed into one who lives for Jesus.

Responding to the Challenge: Has North American self-absorption worked well? Human wreckage is on every side. <u>In conversation and in your work with new believers,</u> <u>contrast Bible-based decisions with those based on self-</u> <u>interest.</u> Make it positive. Never talk about the ugliness of sin without stressing the beauty of salvation. Those who mature into strong Christians are not looking for a slightly prettier pigpen; they want something far different. Are you convinced this Christian life is the best thing going? If you are, then say it by talking about it, singing it, and testifying it... and say it often.

Climate Condition #2 – Biblical Illiteracy

In a recent *Enrichment* article, Greg Ogden wrote, *"Tonight Show* host Jay Leno took to the streets to question people about their Bible knowledge. He approached two college-age women and asked, 'Can you name one of the Ten Commandments?'

Quizzical and blank looks led to this reply, 'Freedom of speech?'

Then Leno turned to a young man and asked, 'Who according to the Bible was eaten by a whale?' With confidence and excitement the guy blurted out, 'I know, I know, Pinocchio.'"[1]

Church Planter Knox Handkins said, "Our new people don't know where the book of Genesis is." You must tell them who David was, explain about Daniel, and tell them... oh yes, tell them all about Jesus and what He has done for them!

Responding to the Challenge: Simplify! Speak at a visitor or new believer's level of understanding, but be constantly lifting the level of Bible knowledge and understanding. One of Paul's instructions regarding a bishop was he was to be, ". . . apt to teach" (1 Timothy 3:2). While this applies most directly to those in a preaching or teaching ministry, as a saint you have a special responsibility to back up the voice of the pastor and encourage your new brothers and sisters in Christ to develop their understanding of the Word.

Additionally, offer help to the new believer struggling to keep up with new Biblical concepts. These days, every text needs to be explained and put in historical perspective. Each Bible character needs an introduction. A minimal level

---

[1] Greg Ogden, "Making Disciples Jesus' Way: A Few at a Time," *Enrichment Journal*, http://enrichmentjournal.ag.org/200801/200801 056_MakeDiscip.cfm.

of Bible knowledge can be assumed. You should expect for new disciples to have a lot of questions about every sermon, and logistically the pastor may not be able to spend time with each newcomer. Come alongside your pastor and help your new brothers and sisters with their <u>basic Bible questions.</u> Be a kind and understanding "big brother" or "big sister" the new babe in Christ can come to after service with their questions.

It will be a failure of the pulpit if the famine of Bible knowledge leads us to "dumb down" Christianity. Historically, the liturgical church and the evangelical movement have followed the pattern of lowering expectations. Their track record does not bode well for those who follow a similar course of action. Why would your new convert want to be part of something that expects nothing of them?

Strategy #1 – Discipleship Classes

A pastor and church intent on, "I travail... until Christ be formed in you," has a plan to develop people. It includes some form of new convert, discipleship, or orientation class.

What is a Discipleship class?

A discipleship class is part of the spiritual nursery: a place for spiritual newborns to be fed. Sirloin steak is good, but it won't benefit a newborn. A lesson on "Justification by Faith" may need to be taught, but the new convert who doesn't know what "justification" is can starve sitting at that table. The new convert has no teeth to sink into the good "meat" you put on the table. New converts need milk.

What makes a Discipleship class effective?

It is taught at the new convert's level of comprehension. This is "pre-school" for Christians. A baby determines the pace of the feeding. Charles Spurgeon said, "Christ said to Peter 'Feed my sheep... feed my lambs.' Some put the food so high that neither lambs nor sheep can reach it. They seem to have read the text, 'Feed my giraffes.'"

A Discipleship class takes into account that most students will take five minutes to find the book of II Corinthians. It slows the teaching process down to accommodate the baby.

How does a Disciples class work?

1. Begin with making it special. Invite every new convert with a personal touch. Send a card or letter... and make it personal. Follow up with a phone call the night before the first class. These simple steps give importance and significance to the process.

2. Make class times convenient for the newcomer rather than convenient for you or someone else. In taking care of babies, there are no convenient times, so you have to be flexible. Remember those late-night feedings? They were never convenient. Adopt a similar mindset with your discipleship classes.

3. In the first class—orient the new person as to what is involved. Give an overview of the curriculum's content and the students' options for growth. In our approach, there were three options:

   - Sitting in the class as a passive participant.

- Participating in the class discussions and interaction. Asking questions and working to discover answers.

- Doing review and preview work at home.

4. Relax—a coat and tie are not essential. In a discipleship class, a podium and platform actually hinder learning. Coffee, donuts, and tea are important. The teacher arriving early to interact with students is important. Quite often the student will ask questions before or after class that they are embarrassed to ask during class.

5. Focus on getting the new saint interacting with the Bible and learning how to have a relationship with the Lord Jesus. Discipleship classes are about the newcomer and their long-term spiritual health. This is not a college professor giving an "information dump" and moving to the next topic. Disciple-makers stay with it until the student understands the content. Where there has been no *learning*, there has been no teaching.

- Student reading and involvement in discussion are important. As they are willing, have the students do all the reading. In the first class I always asked who was willing to read aloud. From that point forward, these people did the reading. The open Bible is the only authority you have.

- Encourage questions. Be willing to say, "I don't know, but I'll try to have you an answer by next week." The answer, "I don't know," eliminates

28

much of the intimidation a student feels.

- Give the student work to do outside of class. This is another way to get them into God's word. This takes two forms: (1) Home work that reviews the last lesson (2) Pre-work that prepares the student for the following week. Every student won't do the review or the pre-work. Those who do the work will grow much quicker. Give those who are interested in quick growth the opportunity to advance.

- All lessons should take the new believers directly to the Bible to see what God says. The Bible needs to be clearly more important than the handouts or workbook.

- At the end of each class, give the student a copy of the more thorough teacher's notes. The teacher's notes help the student complete the home work.

6. Communicate high expectations of your students. From the outset, tell the new convert you imagine them being a Sunday school teacher or eventually teaching the Discipleship class they are now sitting in. A coach who anticipates his team being winners coaches toward a championship. Focus on your winners.

7. Aggressively follow up on absentees. You won't keep many people who do not enter this process. Discipleship classes are "make or break."

What are we to teach the new convert?

Teach toward what you want the person to be. Do you want the disciplines of prayer and God's Word to be important to them? If so, give the new believer resources for prayer and reading the Bible.

[handwritten: witnessing (tell them to share their testimonies)]

Level One focuses on the basic disciplines—prayer, personal devotion, etc. It is almost a variation of the old-fashioned Wesleyan style of training. Level One is oriented toward a method of establishing good habits for the new believer. This level can take four to six weeks.

[handwritten: New Birth why?]

Level Two is doctrinal. We used a self-developed concoction called *Take Root*. This lasted ten weeks. There are many good resources available for you to pick and choose from.

Level Three addresses responsibility. This time the concoction was called *Bear Fruit*. Level three lasted eleven weeks. There are many good resources including: *Ready to Be Free Discipleship Course* ; *My Father's House – Course I and II, My Father's House Mini-Chart, My Father's House in PowerPoint.* All of these new convert curricula are available from HM Sales. Visit http://hmdsales.com or call our toll free number at 1-888-426-8543.

In our efforts, *Level Four* placed the student in a defined role of ministry. We called this particular series *Fitly Framed.* It lasted five weeks. During this time the goal was to advance the person toward becoming a "full corn in the ear."

How can we take Discipleship to the next level?

Little things mean a lot. Celebrate Discipleship graduates in a public setting. Our celebration included students coming to the platform to receive a certificate. I learned from Art Hodges to have a few people coached a bit to clap, cheer, and whistle in celebration.

Often, we'd have one of the new converts volunteer to bring the donuts and another would commit to prepare the coffee. This gives an opportunity to evaluate the newcomers level of "follow-through." Did they make the commitment and then forget? Perhaps they went the second mile.

Don't do shortcuts. Give a fifth grader a diploma calling him a college graduate and he still doesn't have a college education.

If you are responsible to teach a Discipleship class, you cannot go free-lancing. Your Saturday evening dream about dispensationalism or one of Ezekiel's visions may be relevant somewhere, but not in the Discipleship class. The Discipleship classes must stay on point.

"Building a Hothouse" – Implementing the Strategies:

Like the tomato plant, our converts can grow if they have the right environment, or hothouse. Take a moment to assess your church's hothouse.

- Are you doing your part to see that your church presents a positive, life-changing alternative to the self-centered way of the world?

- Are you an inviting friend a new convert would feel comfortable coming to with a question about the Bible or a point in the pastor's sermon?

- Have you offered to assist with a Discipleship class in your church?

- If you are a leader in the class, have you situated it at a convenient time for new converts?

- Does someone make a *personal* invitation to new converts for the class?

- Is the class geared to the level of knowledge of the students?

- Is student-participation encouraged (reading in class, pre-work, and home work)?

- Are you following up on absentees?

- Are you celebrating completion of the class?

Chapter 4:
Disciples: An Intentional Product

"If you don't know where you are going, any old road will get you there!" —Lewis Caroll

Some churches celebrate conversions and report great numbers being born again but never seem to be any larger. No new buildings are ever needed; somehow they stay the same size year after year.

We had a pretty good revival in my home church. It increased the attendance significantly. One of the good men in our church had been through a few cycles of ingathering. Harvey said, "It'll take us six months to get back to normal."

There is a crisis in discipleship. Some call it, "Closing the back door." Bill Hull wrote, "Discipleship making is not *one* of the things a church does. It *is* what a church does."[2] Counting the number baptized or how many received the Holy Ghost should not satisfy. It cannot... it must not. Disciple-making is the program—the *only* program of the church. Children's Ministry should make disciples! Youth

---

[2] Bill Hull, *Pastor's Update*/Volume 48, (Pasadena, CA: Fuller Evangelistic Association).

Ministry should make disciples! Ladies Ministry should make disciples! Men's Ministry should make disciples! In your local church, how well is each of those ministries doing in developing converts into true disciples of Jesus Christ?

Weak disciple-making fits into two major categories: flawed goals and defective approaches. An example of a flawed goal is to set a goal for baptisms but never ask how many of the baptized move on to Christian maturity. A defective approach is to rely on someone's church attendance as the lone measure of one's being a disciple of Jesus. While church attendance is part of the strategy, it is only part of the plan. One can attend church for years and still not be a mature disciple.

Here is where the hard part begins. What are the vital components of a finished product—a finished disciple? Automobiles don't look exactly alike, but some vital components exist in every automobile. Every mature disciple will not be exactly alike, but some things are consistent to every disciple. Recognizing the defining traits of a disciple of Christ may well change our way of doing ministry.

The work product of the church is not good sermons or fine buildings. The work product of the church is not attendees. The work product of the church is not an impressive choir. The work product of the church is not a list of strong programs. One reason Home Missions churches are the most effective action going on is because all energy is focused on the main thing—making disciples.

Disciples are the end product of the church—all of the other nice things I've mentioned are part of the process intended to develop this magnificent end product. When something intended to be a process becomes an end unto itself—"the praise team, the choir, the building"—we've missed the point.

In a Columbus, Indiana, mall there is an elaborate contraption taking up several hundred square feet and standing two stories tall. It is magnificent. Bearings roll, chains clank, gears engage, and a "thing-a-ma-jig" moves. It has operated for decades. What does it produce? Nothing! When everything gets through moving, it has accomplished absolutely nothing. The elaborate contraption was intended by the designer to do what it does: activity without accomplishment. God's church was not so intended. It has an objective: make disciples. So how much of your church's activities actually accomplish something?

If the church were a factory, its sole output would be to make disciples. So how are we doing? One writer argues, "The crisis at the heart of the church is a crisis of product."[3] Disciple is the Greek root word matheo. From matheo we also get our English word math. Math is a rather precise science. The best and most precise math that will add to the church and then multiply the church is through discipleship. Discipleship is a long-term investment that can seem boring compared with the measures some use as the gauge of success.

Disciple-making is no more of a casual thing than the manufacture of an automobile. Workers on an assembly line are not surprised at what rolls off the end of the line. Every action has been intentionally focused on exactly that end product. Labor has been done per the plan. It is an intentional thing with an expected end result.

Disciple makers do things intentionally with a certain result being expected. If that result is not achieved, it is not because we did not give it our best effort.

Non-ostrich churches (mothering churches) do four things:

1. Identify their end product.

---

[3] Bill Hull, The Disciple-making Pastor (Grand Rapids: Revell, 1988), 14.

2. Have a good snapshot of what a disciple looks and acts like.

3. Decide how they plan to move people toward becoming like that snapshot.

4. Establish a setting and appropriate vehicles for developing people.

So what does a disciple of Jesus Christ look like? What are the most outstanding characteristics when one sees the snapshot?

Disciple-making's Three Vital Objectives

Abide in His Word – John 8:31: "So Jesus said..., If you abide in My word, you are truly My disciples" (Amplified).

The word "abide" means to exist in an environment. A plant *abides* in soil. A fish *abides* in water. How would a fish do if it was in water three times each week—Sunday at 10:00 a.m. and 6 p.m. and Wednesday at 7:00 p.m.? Quick answer—dead fish!

A disciple who abides in Jesus' Word reads, studies, and works to personally understand. A disciple's environment for survival is the Word—not just the Word spoken or words spoken about His Word, but the Word itself. A disciple outside the Word is like a fish out of water. He cannot survive. Oh, he may survive as church member or an attendee, but not as a disciple of Jesus.

What does all this mean to one who would be a disciple-maker?

- From the outset, the Bible is held up as THE authority. Any question is answered by THE Word. In answer to the questions and problems of those first disciples, Jesus quoted the Old Testament 160 times.

- From day one, new believers are encouraged, challenged, and taught to read the Bible for themselves. God has magnified His word above His name (Psalm 138:2). It is not what I say about His word that is magnified. His Word is magnified.

Occasionally when preaching, Nona Freeman would ask those who had read the Bible through in the past year to stand. Almost always, those who had read the Bible through were a tiny percentage of the audience. If the lone criteria for being determined to be a disciple of Jesus were time spent abiding in the Word, how would converts (or the entire congregation) fare?

It is mundane and simplistic, but you can't build a skyscraper without a foundation. Jesus' words are the foundation for having an effective life. Do we need to rethink some of this? You can lead a horse to water, but you can't make him drink; however you can salt his hay. Our sermons and Bible studies can become the salt that motivates people to drink from God's Word. Let's incite new converts to abide in God's Word. Some ideas you might put to use:

- Give a new convert a simple pattern to read the Bible at their level of spiritual commitment and follow up with him or her about it. A new believer may not read five chapters a day. Provide a guide for reading one chapter or even one paragraph. One paragraph understood is better than five chapters glanced at. Direct converts to books or passages of particular relevance to a spiritual baby. I John was the first book I had them read—it refers to "little children" quite often. Then on to the Acts of the Apostles. <u>Establishing a discipline for getting into the Word of God is the main thing.</u>

- Give the convert a pattern for thinking through what has been read and finding points of relevance and application for themselves. Warning: this will add to your work. New converts who read the Bible develop questions.

- For teachers: At the weekly Bible lesson, <u>give your audience a handout.</u> It could include some recommendations for follow-up reading.

Plan A.

- For small group leaders: Use Sunday's message as a basis for developing the discussion items for the small group meetings of the following week. This gives new members a chance to talk through what they are learning and have questions answered.

Plan B

- For the social media fans: God's Word should be a basis for meditation. One picks up the flavor of that in which they mentally marinate. "Think on these things" promotes a Biblical perspective of life. Could we provide new disciples <u>a passage of the day</u> on <u>which to meditate?</u> Social media would seem to lend itself to providing such resources.

- For the cyber-savvy: the pastor could have <u>a blog</u> <u>where he provided a paragraph of commentary</u> <u>about the passage of the day.</u> Has God gifted you with an inclination toward technology? Perhaps you could offer to set this up for your pastor?

- For those involved in the services: Make the Bible a primary part of church. The Psalms are praise and worship passages; read aloud they bring prominence to the scripture. For some years, a strong disciple-making church in northern Indiana has begun every service with progressively reading a chapter from the New Testament. Old Testament readings are a key part of worship at any synagogue.

- For preachers: Perhaps I need to evaluate how much Bible I really preach. Do I preach His Word or my opinions about His Word? Is there a thimble full of Bible, a thimble full of Zig Ziglar, a sprinkling of Chesterton, a dash of Louis L'amour, and a gallon of me? In my last ten messages, how many seconds or minutes of Bible were actually in those sermons?

God's Word is the environment for disciple life. It is the pastor's responsibility to get a new convert immersed into an environment where the Word is *the* thing. Preaching is an important step in disciple-making, but it's not enough. As we connect people with God's Word, we equip them to compare God's Word to the world's values.[4] Saints are crucial here in emphasizing the value and necessity of God's Word through conversation and example.

Love One Another – John 13:35: "By this shall all men know that ye are my disciples, if ye have love one to another."

In two verses Jesus gave three points of emphasis:

- The object to be loved – one another.

---

[4] Michael J. Wilkins, "Disciple Making for Changing Times and Changing Churches," *Enrichment*/Winter 2008, 44.

- The measure of that love – like Jesus loved.

- The purpose of the love – that others see and know you to be my disciples.

Disciple-making includes community. Christianity is not at its best in isolation. A vertical relationship with Jesus is always the basis for healthy horizontal relationships. Richard Foster wrote, "The Christian life comes not by gritting our teeth but by falling in love."[5]

We are to fall in love with Him and fall in love with one another. What does that mean? Is it some warm fuzzy feeling? No, love is a behavior. New believers need the opportunity to connect with other people in their new church. I mean the good, bad, and ugly of the church. Realizing the love expressed to those who hurt and those who have damaged themselves becomes the basis for their becoming loving themselves.

Jesus' teaching goes beyond, "Love your neighbor as yourself." He tells His disciples to love as He has loved. Jesus had just demonstrated His love to the disciples by washing their dusty, dirty feet. I doubt the disciple's dirty feet inspired any warm fuzzy feelings. He loved the twelve not because they were so loveable, but because they were in need of so much love.

If there was ever a group that didn't measure up, it was the twelve. Instead of expecting them to conform to some unattainable expectation, Jesus created an environment that brought out the best in the twelve and helped them grow. Four traits dominated His loving them.

---

[5] Richard Foster, *Streams of Living Water* (San Francisco: Harper San Francisco, 1998), 51.

These are patterns for a disciple-making church:

1. Jesus accepted them, even as He worked to make them better.

2. He was open to the disciples. Jesus hung out with them and questions were welcomed and answered.

3. Teamwork: they all worked together toward a common cause.

4. Accountability and an expectation of growth.

Making disciples places a priority on bringing people into relationships, not an invitation to a program. Relationships grow while programs run their course. Do we equip new converts to act in a loving way?

Bearing Fruit —John 15:8: "Herein is my Father glorified, that ye bear much fruit; so shall ye be my disciples."

Fruit contains the seed of reproduction. Paul describes the fruit of the spirit in Galatians 5:22-23: "But the fruit of the Spirit is love, joy, peace, longsuffering, gentleness, goodness, faith, meekness, temperance."
Where the fruit of the spirit resides, there is reproductive power. Reproduction is not complete in the process of fruit. Fruit is the necessary step—from fruit fall seed… from a seed springs another tree. Fruit bearing is never ended simply by the existence of fruit. Herschel Hobbs put the work into perspective, "The work of evangelism is never complete until the evangelized becomes the evangelizer." How many of those who received the Holy Ghost three years ago are now teaching Home Bible Studies? How many of them are involved in winning others

to Jesus Christ. Barnhouse put it, "Activity is no substitute for fruit bearing!"

How do we get people to be fruitful? Immediately involve a new convert in a Home Bible Study—not toward the end of just teaching the spiritual newborn but with the objective of them teaching others. New believers need to be encouraged to get involved with bus routes and child evangelism. Provide them with opportunities to be fruitful and multiply.

If you want to renew the focus on disciple-making, four things must happen:

1. Realize disciple-making is the mission and mandate. If the church were a factory, disciples would be our end product. How is your "factory" doing?

2. Understand Jesus' snapshot of a disciple. We can't develop people if we don't have a measure of what we want a mature believe to actually be and do.

3. Every person in the church needs a similar understanding. If you are the Children's Ministry director, start thinking about how to disciple children. If you're a youth worker, think about whether you are converting young people or discipling them. The program needs to match the mission.

4. Establish a beachhead by being encouraging to those who may attempt to do a fresh thing with a group of brand new people. You can change a culture if you can affect the next generation. Some old staid churches could be forever changed if the pastor quietly but intentionally invested himself in

making disciples of new converts. Your role may be to encourage what he is attempting to do.

Disciple-making is hard work—but it is THE work.

You Wouldn't Want an Ostrich for Your Mama!

Chapter 5:
It's Time to Pick up the Baby

If parents bring a nine-pound newborn home from the hospital, they are thrilled with the strapping, healthy child God has given them. But if their baby still weighs nine pounds three months later, they will visit every doctor around to find out what is wrong.

Allow me a moment of facetiousness. What is the big deal with those parents? Boy, they are sure hard to please. My, my, they had a baby shower... and then sent out birth announcements. They had a baby—what more could they want?

You *know* what they want: for their infant to become a healthy toddler... for the toddler to be a pre-schooler... and then kindergarten... pre-adolescence... teens... college/career... young adulthood.... Anything less causes deep hurt.

Real parents are not just baby-producers, nor are they perpetual child-care providers; over time with a process and some significant effort and cost, parents turn their bundle of joy into an adult. Ideally—a mature adult.

It's nice having babies... it's not nice if they stay babies forever.

45

Discipleship – Travail beyond Conversion

Paul desired the same thing for his spiritual offspring. He wrote, "My little children, of whom I travail in birth again until Christ be formed in you…" (Galatians 4:19). Notice four things:

1. Note his term for those he writes to: "little children"—alive but limited. These people were born again but not yet mature.

2. "I *travail* in birth *again*." I've travailed once on your behalf; now I'm travailing *again*. Paul took this personally. I wonder what the practical reality of the second travail of Paul actually looked like. In this season what does "travail… until Christ be formed in you," look like? Might it be:

    *   Travail of time invested. Mature believers are developed as someone takes time with them. This investment does not have to be a planned event. Great teaching moments come in casual conversation. Yes, there are the late night phone calls as a new convert is seeking God's answer to a life question. Such times are often a sort of travail. The time could be spent on something else—taking care of your kids or spouse, doing a job around the house, evangelizing someone not yet reached with the gospel, choir practice, or fishing, but none of those are "I travail again…."

    *   Travail of energy expended. People drain energy away. Such expended energy cannot then be used elsewhere. The vigor expended on

46

working with spiritual babies is forever gone. Working with new converts takes a lot out of you.

- Travail of money invested. How much money does a parent spend on a child from birth through college? Those who develop new converts into mature saints put money into them— it's a meal here, a CD bought there, a Youth Camp registration... and... and the list goes on and on. Like raising kids, raising converts never ends.

3. "I travail... again *until*" – *Until* is a measurement of time. Paul, how long are you going to put up with those immature believers in Galatia? <u>Until!</u> How long will you keep taking their calls? <u>Until!</u> How long will *you* teach them? <u>Until!</u> "Until" indicates patient determination. Never quit. Are you part of an "<u>until!</u>" church? Determine as a much-needed saint with a kingdom vision: we will work with new converts "until." It takes at least three to five years to bring a new believer to any significant measure of maturity. Sometimes it takes longer. Don't stop. "I travail... again *until*."

4. Paul, you had a great revival in Galatia. Hundreds received the Holy Ghost. What are you travailing about now? Can you almost hear the apostle, "I'm not satisfied, until Christ be formed in you" – Wait a minute Paul, "They received the Holy Ghost. Isn't that enough?" For Paul, birth was not the goal— perpetuating the species was. I'm going to travail for you with a specific goal in mind. I want you to

have: the heart of Christ... the mind of Christ... the hands of Christ... "until Christ be formed in you."

I know this is what we say we are about, but do we really practice this business of travailing till Christ be formed in them? Do we really feel the pain of such an effort? Are we into *theory* rather than *practice*? Am I like the well-to-do couple who had a new baby? They bought a formidable book on child care. It was quite a resource, covering child rearing from "A to Z." One night as the baby wailed, the parents stood by the crib, desperately scanning the index of their new book and eyeing their newborn with apprehension. They heard a voice from the nursery door where their Irish cook stood looking in: "If I was youse," she said, "I'd put down the book and pick up the baby." We need to get beyond theory and _pick up the baby_.

Let me share a couple of practical things to help with this travail:

Experience the Second Travail – in Prayer

Is it a common mistake to stop praying or reduce our prayers for someone after they have been born again?

Jesus spent three good years training Simon Peter. Simon had observed miracles and been present at the transfiguration. He was convinced. Simon had been in the best of Discipleship classes. Still, Peter was imperfect. Jesus envisioned the best from Simon Peter; why Peter had been granted "the keys to kingdom." At the same time, Jesus never lost sight of Peter's flaws.

As Jesus prepared for the crucifixion, he told Simon, "Satan hath desired to have you, that he may sift you as wheat" (Luke 22:31). Jesus' reaction to Satan's desires regarding Peter is in the next verse: "But I have _prayed_ for thee, that thy faith fail not" (Luke 22:32). Jesus could have done anything for Simon—angels were at His disposal. Did Jesus do what He thought was the absolute best thing for any given situation? "I have prayed for thee...."

If we believe in the power of prayer, there should be a regular time of prayer over new believers. Satan desires to sift them. Pray for new believers in their challenges and for God's mercy on their failures.

Experience the Second Travail – Through Edification

A great Bible word no longer in common use is *edify*. To edify is to "build up." Disciple-makers are people builders. Lyndon Johnson said, "Any old mule can tear down a barn; it takes a man of vision to build one."

In carpentry I'd be like President Johnson's "any old mule." I'm better at demolition than construction. Hopefully, the same is not true in dealing with people. Is it possible that the church has too many demolishers and not enough builders?

There are four primary building tools a disciple-making church has available:

- Disciple-making Tool #1— The use of spiritual gifts: "forasmuch as ye are zealous of spiritual gifts, seek that ye may excel to the edifying of the church" (I Corinthians 14:12). New converts benefit much from the "word of wisdom" and the "word of knowledge." In no instance does the operation of a gift of the spirit have to be something "hocus pocus." The new believer may be built up without ever knowing they have been ministered to by one of the gifts of the spirit.

- Disciple-making Tool #2 – Every part of the church service: "when ye come together, every one of you

hath a psalm, hath a doctrine, hath a tongue, hath a
revelation, hath an interpretation. Let all things be
done unto edifying" (I Corinthians 14:26). Let all
things be done to "build up." Perhaps it is a good
idea to step back from the past weekend and ask,
"How did each part of the service build someone
up?"

- Disciple-making Tool #3 — The five-fold ministry is to
  develop people. Those mature saints will then build
  up of the body of Christ: "For the perfecting of the
  saints, for the work of the ministry, for the edifying
  of the body of Christ" (Ephesians 4:12). Apostles,
  prophets, evangelists, pastors, and teachers have in
  their job description to "perfect" or "mature" the
  saints. If the five-fold ministry does not intentionally
  work to mature saints, how will such maturing occur?
  What are you doing to make sure each of those five
  gifts operates in the local church? Dallas' Pastor Tom
  Foster has intentionally connected each of the five
  ministry roles into his church. He is adamant about
  this connection making a huge difference in the
  church's progress.

- Disciple-making Tool #4 — Involvement. A church is
  tight-knit as a result of each person of the body
  being connected. Connection comes as people do
  the part God has given them to fill: "From whom the
  whole body fitly joined together and compacted by
  that which every joint supplieth... maketh increase
  of the body unto the edifying of itself in love"
  (Ephesians 4:16).

Thinking about the Church

<u>Self-assessment:</u>

- ✓ Does your church have a realistic, workable plan for spiritual formation in the people God adds? Are you supporting your pastor in this plan? How recently have you offered to help? How recently have you taken the initiative and encouraged a new disciple in his or her spiritual growth?

- ✓ If you are a leader in a ministry of the church, are you intentionally including those who are comparatively new to the body?

- ✓ Are you and the church prepared to patiently and painfully travail till Christ be formed in the new believer?

- ✓ Do you have a vision for and a commitment to soulwinning and the disciple-making process?

<u>"Picking Up the Baby" – Implementing the Strategies:</u>

- Set aside personal prayer time to travail for "disciples in the making."

- If you are a prayer leader at your church, make sure that there is special corporate prayer time focused on the babes in Christ.

- Is there a time when in a relatively casual environment the newcomer can express a challenge they are dealing with to you?

51

- Are you actively involved in any of your church's efforts to set up Bible studies and Discipleship classes to build a measure of protection and a mature value system in your upcoming disciples?

- Are you consistently investing time in each of your church's growing disciples?

- Have you asked God to show you what you can do personally to accomplish the church's mission of disciple-making?

Chapter 6:
Mama Wasn't an Ostrich

As I've said to the point of redundancy:

- Making disciples for Jesus Christ happens by intentional action.

- Disciple-making is not a "church growth" method. Disciple-making is "growing Jesus' kingdom" and "growing people."

- Making disciples is long-term. It is not a quick-fix. Discipleship strategies are a bit boring when compared with high-profile events. Don't misunderstand—I enjoy breaking an attendance mark as much as anyone. However, event-focused action does not grow people. Events convert the lost and encourage the saints, but they do not develop leaders. Disciple-making, however, does.

- Disciple-making grows servant-ministers in contrast to attendees. Disciple-making is the process by which one develops leaders. The downside to "events"

53

being the primary strategy—note the word
"primary"—is it leaves a pastor constantly looking for
laborers and leaders.

Any pastor or church that makes a lasting impact has been in
the business of making disciples whether it called it that or not.

Remember the birth of your child or grandchild? During the
escalating intensity of labor, nurses have been in and out of
the room. The doctor has visited. Vital signs of mother and
infant are constantly monitored.

Roll the clock ahead a bit... the baby has just been
born. There is a bustle of activity in the delivery room. A
newborn must be taken care of. There are measurements to
take and statistics to record. Grandparents and close family
make a quick visit. Pictures are taken. A nurse reminds the
new mother of her responsibility of feeding and caring for
the little one. Those moments begin a cycle of ongoing care,
which continues for years to come.

Several websites show that more effective prenatal
and postnatal care have decreased the U.S. infant mortality
rate from 165 deaths per 1,000 births to 7 per 1,000 in
the past 100 years. How babies are born has not changed
since time began. What has changed? The level of prenatal and post-natal care.

Parents and grandparents don't feel discouraged
because only one baby was born. In reality, even if a
particular hospital has a dozen babies born in a single day,
each delivery is individual. These happen one at a time.
Each infant is provided care in an individual way.

Now, imagine the altar and baptismal tank as the
church's delivery room. What happens when there is a
spiritual birth in your church? Do we hug the new baby,
show them to a changing room, and say, "Hope to see you
next week?" Is the new birth briefly celebrated and then

54

ignored? Think back—if you were a spiritual newborn just having received the Holy Ghost, what would you like to happen? Let me offer a thought—one we used to good effect for almost fifteen years.

Nursery Care – Altar Counselors

What if a trained altar counselor met with each one who was baptized or received the Holy Ghost? Just as the nurse is there to expertly handle a new baby, an altar counselor could be on hand to provide specialized care for this youngest of new saints. Think of how it might happen:

1. The altar counselor meets the new believer as they come out of the baptistery changing room or the altar area. The altar counselor takes the initiative, introducing himself or herself to the new convert and explaining that the pastor has asked them to share some things about the church.

2. The altar counselor would guide the new convert to an office or room designated for this purpose. Christian Life Center in Stockton, California, has a room designated for such purposes.

3. A Home Missionary will likely have to serve as his or her own altar counselor. Counsel may have to be provided on a couple of chairs in a corner of the rented meeting room.

An Ideal Altar Counselor

1. A self-starter who can accept responsibility without consistent prompting. If the person is assigned to serve, they need to get the job done.

2. Somewhat outgoing in personality. Part of an altar counselor's role is relationship-building. The assignment to handle this responsibility cannot be viewed as a "must do" thing. If the altar counselor is wishing to be at Taco Bell with a friend, the counseling session will be negative rather than positive.

3. Ideal altar counselors see themselves as delivery room nurses who get to connect to, touch, and ensure the health of a brand new baby.

Saint, you are to be commended for the work you do altar counseling, driving a Sunday school bus, or cleaning the church. The little-seen parts of the body are vital to health.

Vital Statistics

A delivery room nurse is also in the business of vital statistics. The nurse measures and weighs the new baby. Footprints and handprints are taken. Parental information is gathered. The baby's new name is recorded.

Ever read a news account of a hospital losing a baby? Or perhaps giving an infant to the wrong mother? Hospitals have become paranoid about "losing babies." Do we feel the same way? Think about it:

*   Do you know the names of the spiritual babies who have been born during the past year?

*   Do you have the new convert's address, phone number, and email address? Have you ever lost a baby? Simply couldn't find them?

- What is their level of health—in essence, are they in a Home Bible Study? Who are the person's friends in the church?

- Is the baby ready to be nourished? This nourishment likely needs to come through an orientation or new convert's class. Perhaps a more important question—is "mama" ready to feed a baby?

Thus, an altar counselor has vital statistics to gather. In this instance it is not length and weight. Important data includes the new person's name, address, phone numbers, and e-mail address, and certainly information regarding the Home Bible Study (HBS). If the new believer is not involved in a HBS, who can teach them? How quickly can the two people be connected to each other?

Misplaced or unused knowledge is as useless as information one does not have access to. Who gets the vital statistics? Pastor, discipleship director, Home Bible Study teacher, and those who minister to an age group. There are some suggestions later about how to communicate this information.

Resources for a New Convert

The altar counselor is not an inquisitor. They also provide resources to the newcomer. This welcome packet should include at a minimum:

- Phone numbers—the altar counselor, the church, the discipleship director, and pastor.

- Information regarding the church website.

- The church's schedule and specific information about the new convert's class.

- Specific information about children, youth ministry, and the nursery, if applicable.

The following resources could be included to great benefit:

- A book welcoming the new believer. If the pastor can write a book or booklet, it would be wonderful. In our case we used a book based on something I'd taught our church, *The Daily Things of Christian Living*.

- Provide a prayer clock and a CD of the pastor giving the new disciple instructions on how to pray the prayer clock. Your new convert will not pray an hour each day. If you can get them praying twelve or fifteen minutes each day, there has been progress.

- Consider developing a model on how to read a chapter of the Bible to gain the greatest benefit and providing it as a handout to your new converts.

- Provide a listing of gospel radio stations the new believer might be interested in. Satan uses song lyrics to drive home his message. A new believer should be introduced to a different message.

- Apostolic music. If the church has a music project, this CD can be given to the new believer.

- Take a celebratory picture of the new convert. A copy can be given to the new believer. At Pastor

Elias Limones' church in Pittsburg, California, one wall contains pictures of all the new converts of a particular year.

These varied resources can be put into a three-ring binder or a packet.

Making It Work

Some practical things can help make this work. Put the packets together before they are needed. Have copies of the altar counselor's report already made.

Churches of every size can benefit from having a place for central communication. Create a group of mailboxes or cubbyholes to get information from one person to another. If a church can establish a process to communicate this information electronically, it will be even better.

Vital statistics should be entered into a spreadsheet.

For there to be any benefit, there MUST be regularly scheduled review by the pastor with the discipleship director. This weekly or monthly review should include a line-by-line review of the status of every new convert.

Bishop Kenneth Haney shared a key to their growth in Stockton, "We didn't let anybody slip through the cracks. If somebody missed both services on Sunday, by our staff meeting early the following week, somebody needed to be able to let me know where they were at and why they were missing."

Questions must be asked and answered:

• Where is _____?

• Is he attending a Discipleship class?

- What can we do to help get him in a Discipleship class?

- Have you talked with him?

This is hard work, and this sort of effort is systematic. Like a hospital dealing with babies, this work will never end. If you are in the business of making disciples, you and your church will never outgrow this work. You or someone you train has to do it from now on. There is no emotion—just practical plodding work.

Chapter 7:
The Body of Christ Has No Appendix

After generations of study, physicians still have not come up with a viable reason for the appendix to be part of the human body. I have survived and even thrived after having my appendix removed. It appears I could take it or leave it—my body simply did not require an appendix to function. I'm fully aware that we do not yet know all God designed or intended for the human body. In all likelihood there are things we don't yet know about the appendix. It is simply an observation about the church needing every single part and every person.

Paul used the term "body" to describe the church in at least four epistles. His emphasis included:

- Diversity of parts makes up a single body.

- Each diverse part has a distinct function. Each component is needed for the body to be complete.

- The unity of the body—even in its diversity of parts.

61

- No part of the body would treat another part with disdain.

Paul spoke of the foot, hand, ear, eye, nose, head, uncomely parts, and comely parts. Ever noticed—even as he talked about "uncomely parts," Paul did not mention the appendix? Might it be that every single person in the body of Christ is intended to play some significant and meaningful role?

Now think with me a bit... who is the appendix of your local church body? Is there someone who could be removed from that local church without impairing a single ministry? (Being present to help gravity keep a chair in place does not count as having a ministry.) For the sake of thought, take it beyond the financial impact of various attendees—those whose sole contribution is financial.

Is it just me... or do many local church bodies seem to have multiple appendices? Members of the body who seem to fulfill no significant function. Those people who, if surgically removed, would not be missed—because no function of the body would be impaired.

If so, it is a shame, for it is in contrast to the model of the early church. The truth is that the body of Christ—the church—has no unnecessary parts.

We do need people to fill seats. Home Missionaries usually start with "warm bodies." Sunday and midweek attendance numbers are important. However, at least as meaningful is the involvement of those who attend. Are people actually serving? Do they have a ministry? At the end of each week, who or what have they impacted in a specific way?

Are the "doers" around your church perpetually over-worked? Does the way we "do" our church services resemble a sporting event, where a few dash madly about doing everything while the majority sit in the bleachers? Is being part of the church a spectator event rather than a participant event? Are you a warrior or a watcher?

A Pastor's Wake Up

Was it Jesus' plan that His church be a collection of the uninvolved? The late Quaker Elton Trueblood wrote, "Perhaps the greatest single weakness of the contemporary Christian Church is that millions of supposed members are not really involved at all and, what is worse, do not think it strange that they are not.... There is no chance of victory in a military campaign if ninety percent of the soldiers are untrained and uninvolved. Most alleged Christians do not understand that loyalty to Christ means sharing personally in His ministry." Does Trueblood's statement resonate with anyone? It hits home with me.

I've noted that three keys exist to discipling new people:

1. Teach and train them at the level of their understanding.

2. Provide fellowship that develops new friendships.

3. Involve the new believer in a meaningful way. The late David Gray said, "Use them or lose them!" It still holds true.

The church can be a storage unit in which the gift and potential of human resources become dusty and rusty. Could church be a place where people discover their gifts and passions? What if they then mobilized those resources for God's work?

Think specifically about the people who have been saved in the past five years: (1) How many of them are still around? (2) How many of the converts are maturing disciples of Jesus? Three things Jesus said defined His disciples: abiding in God's Word, showing love one to another, and bearing fruit. (3) How many of those saved over the past five years now have a functional role of ministry within the church body?

Just an observation to do with as you will: It is interesting how easy we find a place to put a transferring saint to work, while new additions to the body languish and eventually die.

Let me share my experience...

- One Sunday, I asked myself, "How many of the crowd at Truth Tabernacle—those who call this 'my church'—are active in a defined role of ministry? They consistently serve in some capacity and would be missed if they did not serve?"

- The next day, I went through the church directory asking the same question. To my dismay, _only 18%_ of those who called Truth Tabernacle home were consistently engaged in a defined role of service.

- The disappointing answer to my question started a process of stretching me. It involved study about how "body ministry" is supposed to work and a discovery of the many under-valued and under-appreciated gifts referenced in the Bible.

- The study and discovery resulted in an adjustment in philosophy as to what mattered most. Sunday attendance numbers did not become insignificant, but they became only *part* of the equation. A crowd of uninvolved spectators does not fulfill the definition of a church.

- Results: it was not a quick change, but in time our level of involvement increased. Eventually 62% of those who called Truth Tabernacle their church had a defined role of ministry.

Why So Many Appendices?

We allow people to be guilty of spiritual embezzlement if they rob the Lord of the use of their talents and abilities. If what I've discussed describes your church and piques your interest, it is probably important to think about how we got here. If this is not the way Jesus planned for His church to function, then how did we get to this place?

- We've not been taught about every person having a role of ministry. In my upbringing, one gift and calling was validated. It was the call to be a preacher. Those who volunteered to clean the church were not validated and affirmed as accomplishing a significant ministry for Jesus Christ.

- North American consumerism. People connect to church because of "what's in it for me," rather than as a place to become a servant for Christ. Many *consume* ministry as opposed to *supplying* ministry. Churches have not been measured by ministry participation but by attendance.

- Challenging people without giving them a path to follow. I had given lip-service to "every man a ministry," but I did not fully grasp its application. If I say, "Go win souls," or "Do something for God," without equipping the person to fulfill that directive, I've created festering frustration and demotivated them. Mapping paths to service for new believers is

65

hard work.

- Is it possible I was insecure about empowering saints to make decisions and take actions? Did I (or more often Norma, my oft over-laden wife) have to be the one who went to Office Depot to purchase supplies? What compulsive behavior requires me to have to be the one who gets the mail? Insecurity prompts overt control.

- We did not have a structure to discover people's abilities. Sitting on pews were men and women with specialized skills who eventually made the church so much more effective. Nor have we had a process by which we could connect people and their gifts to the right place to serve.

- Developing people was much harder than baptizing them. For some years we baptized quite a few but did not really have much growth. When our Discipleship process began to include the expectation of every single person having a functional ministry, we moved forward. A professor described one under-achieving student as having a great gift, but being too lazy to unwrap it. Were there gifts God provided to our church that I was too lazy to unwrap and put to use? Creating consistent processes that move people toward involvement is hard work. We tend to like the quick-fix. Activating inactive people and new converts is not a quick-fix.

Unfortunately, research says my statistics regarding involvement were actually beyond the norm. A survey by pollster George Barna said that as little as ten percent of

Christians actually do the work in the local church. The question is, "What are we going to do about it?"

Getting a Head Start on Increasing Involvement

1. Consider your involvement at your church. Are you doing all you can to serve and is there a way you can involve new disciples in what you do?

2. Think about the following and answer the questions (even if you don't like the answers): How does someone move from being a new convert to being on the church cleaning staff? Where would a newcomer go to learn about it? How might a new convert become part of the choir? How might that same person be developed to eventually be the leader of a praise team? Choir Director? Music Director? What process is there for intentionally developing people toward having a ministry? How would a new convert be equipped to teach Home Bible Studies? To lead a team of teachers? To become a "Staff Evangelist" doing follow-up and teaching Home Bible Studies? If the answer to the questions is a bit unclear, it may indicate a breakdown in having processes to disciple people, discover their gifts and talents, and fully develop their capabilities.

3. How many of those converted five years ago are actively involved in a defined role of ministry? What can you do to encourage them to get involved?

4. Acquire "Fitly Framed." These seven lessons help people find their place of service.

5. Read Don and Katie Fortune's book: *Discover Your God-given Gifts.*

Envision the possibilities of every member in your church having a role—an *active* role. Paul reminded us that we are the body of Christ and members in particular; the body of Christ has no non-essential parts. The body of Christ has no appendix!

Chapter 8:
You Won't Keep Them All

In *Building High Commitment in a Low Commitment World,* Bill Hull wrote, "My experience has shown that where high commitment is taught as normal, as many as 50 to 65 percent will achieve it." If Hull is correct:

What happens where low commitment is the norm?

Mark, Chris, Margie, Jim, Steve, Tiny, Karen, Amber, Wanda, Jerry, Heather, Becky, Brad, Monique, Terry, Doug, Linda, Pam, Teri, Daniel, Robert, Nicole, Brandon, Anthony, Trudy—these names don't mean much to you, but they mean much to me.

They are some of my failures. That isn't all of them. Hundreds more are on the list—born again but not discipled.

I seem to have a problem. The list of those who <u>did not</u> become disciples is considerably longer than the list of those who <u>did</u>. I'm a mess.

Of course, by church growth measures, Jesus was a failure. He had attracted a crowd of over 3,000. He then talked about the cross. Jesus' audience shrunk to twelve. I've lost people, but never at quite that pace.

Jesus' approach was unusual. A rich, young man asked, "What must I do to inherit eternal life?" Jesus responded with some references to Moses' teachings. The man replied, "These I've kept since I was a boy." Jesus raised the bar, "Sell everything you have and give to the poor" (Mark 10:17-22). The fellow went away. Several things to note:

- Jesus did not renegotiate expectations. He let the rich, young ruler leave.

- Jesus did not change His expectations based on a person's place in society. In reality, the rich, young ruler's assets were his idol. When idols are made an issue, many join the rich young ruler and walk away.

- The rich, young ruler was willing to be a convert, but not willing to pay the price of discipleship. He wanted religion that was convenient, but not one that affected his comfort. Many of my "failures" were a modern version of the rich young ruler.

Jesus dealt with things in such a way that people had to make a decision. Jesus had high expectations. If someone did not want to live up to those high expectations, He was totally willing to let them walk away.

No church keeps everyone, and leadership chooses who you lose. Knowing you won't keep every convert does not excuse giving it your best effort. Disciple-making should be the focus of EVERY ministry in the church, but even then you won't keep them all.

As a frustrated novice pastor, Jeff Ralston phoned his mentor Marrell Cornwell. Perhaps having received a word from the Lord, Bro. Cornwell said, "Let the backslider backslide," and hung up.

What Does Harvest Look Like?

In Jesus' era, you gathered sheaves. Sheaves were taken to a threshing floor. It took time and effort to turn an ingathering into a useable harvest.

1. On the threshing floor, an ox walked on the sheaves, breaking the grain from the stalk. The broken stalks were swept aside.

2. What survived the breaking process was tossed up while a large hand-fan stirred the air. The fan blew the "fluff" away. What the fan did not blow away fell to the threshing floor. Most of what now lay on the threshing floor was grain—not fodder or fluff.

3. The remainder, which was only a minute part of the original ingathering, was shaken through a sieve to filter away the tiny particles of chaff.[6]

What remained was available to plant for future harvest, or to be put to use at the dinner table. If there is no winnowing process, the good grain was as of little use as the stalks or the chaff—not good for bread or reproduction.

Luke 14 records three negative remarks regarding discipleship. Jesus said you can't be His disciple if you don't:

1. Love me more than your family (v. 26)

---

[6] Chester Wright, Maryland/DC District Superintendent, Superintendent's Message at Maryland/DC District Conference, May 2008. Used with permission.

2. Take up your cross daily and follow me (v. 27)

3. Give up your own personal idolatry (v. 33)

Jesus *intentionally* eliminated the stalks and chaff from the wheat. Jesus had 3,000 attendees, but after a process, He had twelve disciples. Breaking, shaking, and sifting divided the useable from the gathered. Until new converts go through the threshing floor, you never know what you really have.

This is a challenge for some of us. We measure significance by the number who gather to worship. "You can always get a crowd, if you demand very little and put on a show."[7] The attendance assessment is weak. It is flawed because it does not ask, "How many of these people are committed?" Sunday is a poor measure of commitment. Commitment is measured by calendar and check book. Mid-week, small group attendance, consistent involvement in the church's prayer program, having an active ministry role in the church, and the giving report are better tools for evaluating the number of disciples. Bringing people to these commitments becomes a threshing floor for new believers.

I'm not espousing the "fewer and purer." I've a picture standing before a church sign directing one to *The Faithful Few Apostolic Church/Victory Tabernacle*. That isn't our goal: we teach people as spiritual babies, develop them, grow them, and keep them coming at their level of commitment.

Part of a pastor's job is to teach Bible principles that oppose the flesh. Those principles separate. The rich young ruler made a decision. If it took selling all, then he was unwilling to stay. The path was too difficult. Our work is not necessarily to be the most popular bunch in town. We must not be, ". . . proliferators of self-indulgent consumer religion,

---

[7] Bill Hull. *The Disciple Making Pastor* (Grand Rapids, Revell Books, 1999) 21.

the what-can-the-church-do-for-me syndrome."[8] With that approach the fluff and fodder stay in place to ever limit the effectiveness of the wheat.

But it cannot be simply the pastor's job. You, faithful saint, are called to back up your pastor's preaching and encourage your new brothers and sisters as they walk through the threshing floor experience.

The Threshing Floor

A convert arrives at the threshing floor. What happens? Christianity is counter-cultural. New people quickly see that. Proclaim the Scriptures' absolute right to direct life and people leave. The simplest Bible teaching—morality, honesty, or giving a good day's work for the employer's pay—is contrary to society.

Discipleship gives people a reason to change behavior as the Bible demands that behaviors change. For example, racial prejudice has to be abandoned—the Bible says so. When a new convert hears that, some decide to take the step of abandoning racism, others are not so willing and go away.

Reproducing saints are separated from the "stuff" in the activity of the threshing floor. The breaking comes a bit at a time. Battles over prayer, Bible reading, faithfulness to attend church, the tithe, and dressing modestly all become places of decision.

Post-modern culture has decreed everything to be relative—without absolutes. In 1986 the World Council of Churches changed their motto to, "The world sets the agenda for the church." Apply that view to what disciples are to become, and normal Christian living is soon defined

---

[8] Ibid.

by what church-goers practice, rather than what the Scripture teaches.

Can *normal* Christian living be downgraded to accommodate culture? Is the belief that the typical saint will be highly committed to the cause of Christ out of vogue?

What today's church culture calls *normal*, Jesus considered *disobedient*. Might I be so driven to succeed that I put the stalks and chaff in the barn along with the good grain? It makes for a fuller barn, but in time rot sets in and I lose the useable grain.

The Un-disciple-able

You need to know the ones you won't keep. Some of them:

1. The unteachable – Paul's instruction to Timothy to "preach the word... reprove, rebuke, exhort with all longsuffering and patience" was based on there being those only interested in hearing those who would scratch their itching ears (II Timothy 4). Some will not be taught. We never had ONE... not even one productive saint whom we could not get into a Discipleship class.

2. The uncommitted – These are there when you see them, but do not accept any sort of consistent demand on them. They *may* come for the occasional extra activity such as a work-day and *may* give to a special needs offering, but call them to dedicate to a consistent weekly effort, and they are blown away like chaff.

3. The unconvinced – God's word is good, so long as it does not meddle into my lifestyle.

4. Those who anxiously reach for blessings but are immature. These can be some of the most active while the music is playing, but seem petrified into inactivity by an approaching usher.

Faithfulness is the rite of passage to meaningful Christianity. Various organizations have traditions that make it possible for new members to advance. The Israeli Army requires all soldiers to run up the historic Masada at night with a torch in hand. They stand in the darkness above the Dead Sea and sing Israel's national anthem. It is not the first requirement to be an Israeli soldier, but eventually all soldiers make that run. It is not an option. A journey to faithfulness is each convert's process and commitment is the torch they must bear. It is not a convert's *first* thing, but it is a necessary thing.

My standards were high. No person helped in a Sunday school class until they'd graduated from our second level of discipleship. A convert would have been at the church for six months. They had enough in them to not be broken or blown away by those twenty-one classes. It allowed them to make decisions about their level of commitment.

Principles to Take Away

1. Know what wheat looks like. Distinguishing between fodder and grain and deciding what you want to keep should be obvious. By the way—you won't keep them both. If you want to accommodate everything in culture, the real grain won't stay.

2. Have a Bible-based process. Let the process develop people. Let the process separate people. In this process, elevate God's Word to its place of

authority.

3. Have high expectations of people. Jesus did. Teach to those expectations and don't compromise those ideals for leaders or teachers.

4. Be doctrinal. Some say, "To be relevant we cannot be doctrinal." Wrong—right practice is always derived from right doctrine. It is impossible to be practical without being doctrinal. Doctrine is the foundation for the practical.

5. Patiently eliminate real issues: deceitfulness of riches, cares of life, and lust for other things.

6. Lose people for the right reason and never because they were not given proper care.

7. Let the backslider—backslide!

8. Have a process to then turn good grain into something useful and useable.

Conclusion

We may not keep them all, but we must try. The church *cannot* be an ostrich! Whether pastor, discipleship director, or faithful saint—it takes the whole church. We *all* must accept the vision for discipleship, commit to working together to help transform our churches into nests, and actively care for the babes God gives us.

Appendix:
Helpful Resources

The documents provided on the following pages can be used to assist the local church in establishing successful disciple-making processes.

Weekly Report

CONFIDENTIAL REPORT FOR _____ (week)

Name	Baptized (Date)	Received Holy Ghost	Attendance this month	Home Bible Study (Y/N)	Level 1 Discipleship (Start – Finish)	Level 2 Discipleship (Start – Finish)	Fellowship Assignment	Church Involvement & Activity

Altar Counselor Report

Personal Information   Date:
Name:
Address:
Home Phone:

Altar Counselor Report   Yes   No
Did you discuss:

      Repentance   ____   ____

      Baptism in Jesus' name   ____   ____
      Date Baptized in Jesus' name:

      Holy Ghost infilling   ____   ____
      Date Baptized in Jesus' name:

      Faithfulness to church   ____   ____

      Bible reading   ____   ____

      Prayer   ____   ____

      Expected reaction of friends/family ____   ____

Did you:

      Invite convert to Sunday   ____   ____
      morning Christian Development class

      Give packet to convert   ____   ____

End this session with prayer!

_____
                          Altar Counselor's Signature

DO NOT WRITE BELOW THIS LINE:
Name of spiritual parent: Spiritual parent's phone #:
Name of phone friend: Phone friend's phone #:
Certificate type?   Baptism / Holy Ghost
Data in computer for letter?   Yes / No

Altar Counselor Job Description

SUMMARY OF AUTHORITY AND RESPONSIBILITY: To obtain information about the new convert at the altar and counsel them, assisting them in their new walk.

DUTIES INCLUDE:

1. Praying with prospective new converts at the altar.

2. Introducing oneself to the new convert whom the New Convert Care Director assigns (assigned for the purpose of counseling with and get acquainted with the new convert).

3. Prepare a New Convert Report.

4. Counsel the New Convert one-on-one going through the prepared check list. This will be done in an assigned room in a comfortable setting.

5. Give the New Convert the prepared packet and any other material so assigned.

6. Contact the New Convert within two days by telephone or a personal visit.

7. Place all paperwork in the designated area for the New Convert Care Director.

8. Be an example in prayer and praise, church attendance, and bringing guests to church. God loves faithfulness.

ACCOUNTABLE TO: New Convert Care Director

EVALUATION:
Quarterly by the Pastor and Director. We will jointly assess any changes that may be needed in the job description, as well as additional personnel that may be required.

I HAVE READ THE JOB DESCRIPTION AND UNDERSTAND ITS RESPONSIBILITIES AND THE THINGS FOR WHICH I AM ACCOUNTABLE.

I AM COMMITTED TO SERVING IN THIS CAPACITY TO THE BEST OF MY ABILITY.

_____
SIGNATURE

I COMMIT MYSELF TO OFFERING THE SUPPORT AND GUIDANCE NECESSARY FOR YOU TO DO THE JOB TO WHICH YOU HAVE COMMITTED YOURSELF. I HAVE UTMOST CONFIDENCE IN YOUR ABILITY TO DO THE TASK WHICH HAS BEEN DELEGATED TO YOU.

_____
SIGNATURE

Defined Paths for Disciple-making

The following churches use defined paths—intentional discipleship models. Visit their websites for more information.

Kent Elliott
Faith Tabernacle
Manchester, CT
http://www.faithtabernacle.com/

Knox Handkins
New Life Christian Center
Exton, PA
http://www.newlifeforme.cc/

Anthony Mangun
The Pentecostals of Alexandria
Alexandria, LA
http://www.thepentecostals.org/

Points of Celebration

Remember to celebrate the special milestones in a growing disciple's journey. The following diagram illustrates key opportunities:

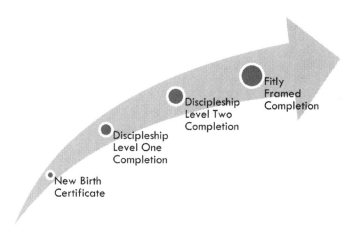

At each of these points, publicly acknowledge the disciple's progress. What gets celebrated gets repeated.

83086043R00048

Made in the USA
Columbia, SC
08 December 2017